Contents

Foreword 2

The game 3

The field 3
  Playing areas and markings 5

Equipment 8
  Sticks 8
  Ball 8
  Uniform 8

Rules of play 10
  Duration of game 10
  Choice of ends 10
  Starting and restarting the game 10
  Ball in and out of play 11
  The push-/hit-in 11
  16 yard hit-out 13
  A push or hit from the back line 14
  Scoring a goal 14

Fouls 15
  Dangerous play 15
  Backsticks 16
  Interference 16
  Handling the ball 17
  Interfer... stick 18
  Goalkeeper's privileges 19

Offside 20

Penalties 22
  Penalty stroke 23
  Penalty corner 25
  Free hit 27

Control of the game 28
  Umpires 28
  Timekeepers 30
  Technical tables 31

Questions 32

Index inside back cover

Foreword

This publication has proved to be one of the most popular produced by the All England Women's Hockey Association. It covers all aspects of the game, coaching, umpiring, and the skills required by the young players of today. The clear illustrations, together with explanations of the rules, mean that all interested in hockey will find it invaluable. I recommend it unreservedly.

'Hockey is going places'—I am sure this book will help you to come along with us.

Barbara L. Holland
President, A.E.W.H.A.

Acknowledgements
Thanks to all who have contributed to this edition, especially Audrey Appleby, Barbara Ashworth, Joan Davies, Doreen Henry and Budge Stuart Smith.

Photographs—Eileen Langsley (cover, pp.1, 2, 6, 12, 14, 16, 23, 24, 25, 31, 32); Hockey Field magazine (inside cover, pp.13, 18, 19); David Hewitson (pp.15, 17, 26, 27, 29)

A good tackle—the player (right) is well ahead and there is no danger of obstruction

The game

Hockey is a very old game. There are records that a stick game rather like hockey was played by the Persians, Greeks and Romans. Modern hockey was introduced into England about 1875; the Hockey Association was formed in 1886 and the All England Women's Hockey Association was formed in 1895. The game remains one of the few purely amateur sports.

Hockey is played between two teams of eleven players. A team may have only one goalkeeper on the pitch at any time; there is no other restriction on the formation adopted. Originally, all teams played with five forwards, supported by three halves and two backs, with the goalkeeper as the last line of defence. Gradually, however, other systems have evolved, leading to a variety of more flexible formations, with players usually classified simply as attackers or defenders, and taking up positions worked out with the coach during training.

Another member of the team may change roles with the goalkeeper during the match, provided the umpire is notified. It is also courteous to notify the opposing captain if the change is made during half-time.

Two substitutes are normally permitted, although this may be increased for certain tournaments, in which case it will be stated in the regulations covering the event.

The substitutes may be introduced with the umpire's permission at any stoppage other than for a penalty corner or a penalty stroke. A player, once substituted, may take no further part in the game.

The aim of the game is to score goals by sending the ball between the goal posts, the ball having been struck by the attacking team in the goal circle. The ball may only be hit with the stick, and may not be kicked, or thrown, or propelled by any part of the body.

The field

Dimensions and size

The size of the field can make a great deal of difference to the standard of play. If the field is too small the players will be crowded and good forward play and accurate movements from one player to another will be impossible. *The Code of Rules for the Game of Hockey* states that the field should be 100 yards long and 60 yards wide, though for young players a small pitch is advocated, e.g. 55–60 yards long and 40–50 yards wide, when Mini or Junior 7-a-side hockey is being played. Clubs should do their utmost to see that their fields are full-size.

The surface of the field should be kept level, close cut and well rolled. The white marking should be 3 inches (7.6 cm) wide, and all stones or other dangerous obstructions should be removed.

All-weather and artificial turf pitches are permissible; there is increasing use of these surfaces.

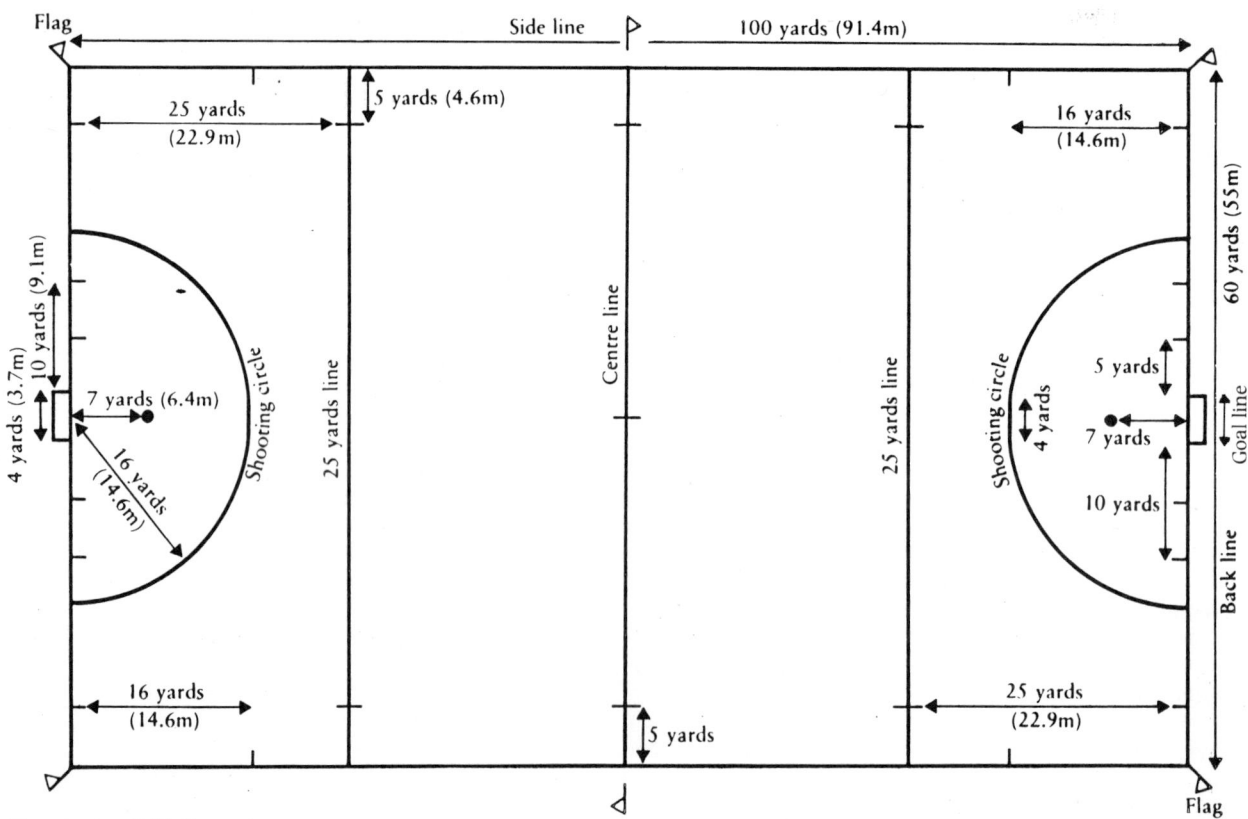

The playing field dimensions

Playing areas and markings

The centre line indicates the division of the field into two equal halves for the purpose of:

(a) Pass-back—when all players except the striker must be in their own half of the field until the ball is in play;

(b) Penalty corner—when six of the defending team must be beyond the centre line until the ball is struck;

(c) Umpiring—each umpire has control of that half of the field which is on her right hand side, when she is standing at the halfway line, facing the centre.

The side lines mark the width boundaries of the field. When the whole ball, off the stick of a player, passes out of play over either of these side lines, a push-in or hit-in is taken by a player of the team opposed to that of the player who last touched it.

The back lines are the lines at each end of the field, joining and at right angles to the side lines.

The portion in front of the goal mouth is called the 'goal line'.

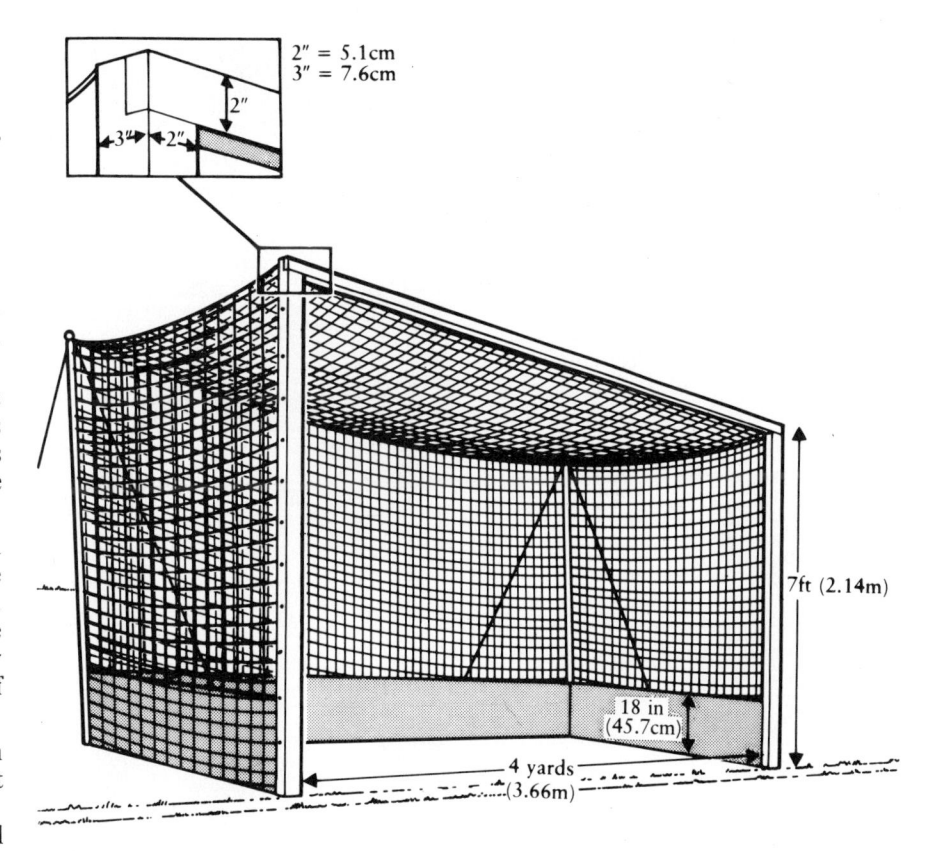

Goal measurements

2" = 5.1cm
3" = 7.6cm

7ft (2.14m)
18 in (45.7cm)
4 yards (3.66m)

When the whole of the ball passes over the goal line or back line, either on the ground or in the air, and a goal is not scored, the ball is out of play. The game is restarted by:

(a) A 16 yards hit-out—if the ball was last hit by an attacker or in the opinion of the umpire, was last hit unintentionally by a defender from a distance of 25 yards or more from the back line;

(b) A push or hit from the back line—when the ball has glanced off the stick of a defending player, or if she unintentionally hits the ball over the back line from within the 25 yards area;

(c) A penalty corner—if a defending player intentionally hits the ball over the back line from within the 25 yards area.

The goal line in front of the posts serves to show that when the whole of the ball has passed over the line, and under the cross-bar, a goal has been scored, unless otherwise provided for by the rules.

American and New Zealand players compete for possession of ball ▶

The goals
The goals are placed in the centre of each back line and behind each goal line, and consist of two perpendicular posts, 4 yards (3.66 m) apart, joined together by a horizontal cross-bar, 7 feet (2.14 m) from the ground. The two posts and the cross-bar should be 2 inches wide and not more than 3 inches deep (5.1 × 7.6 cm). The sides of the posts and cross-bar which face the field should be flat, not curved.

Nets should be firmly fixed to the posts and cross-bar and to the ground behind the goals so that there is no gap for the ball to pass through.

Boards, 18 inches (45.7 cm) in height, shall be placed at the foot of the goal net, the shorter boards being at right angles to the goal line. These boards should be painted a dark colour.

Shooting circle
In front of each goal is a white line four yards long, parallel to, and 16 yards from, the back line. This line is continued to meet the back line by two quarter circles, each with a goal post as centre. The space enclosed by these lines is the shooting circle. It serves the following purposes:

(a) Indicates the area in which a forward may score a goal;
(b) Indicates that part of the field where the goalkeeper may kick the ball;
(c) Indicates the area outside which all attacking players (their sticks and feet) except the striker must be when a penalty corner is being taken;
(d) Indicates that part of the field in which a penalty corner is awarded for an unintentional foul committed by a defending player;
(e) Indicates the area in which a penalty stroke may be awarded for an intentional foul by a defender or for a defence foul which prevents a probable goal;
(f) Indicates the area into which the ball must not be lifted deliberately.

Flag post

25 yards area
The 25 yards area is a rectangle 55–60 yards by 25 yards (*i.e.* the width of the field and 25 yards from the back lines). The 25 yard lines are unbroken right across the field. They serve the following purposes:

(a) To indicate that part of the field in which, if the ball glances off the stick of a defender over the back line, or is hit unintentionally over the back line by a defender, a push or hit from the back line is awarded;
(b) To indicate the area outside which all players must stand for a penalty stroke, except the two players taking part in this;
(c) To indicate the area in which a penalty corner may be awarded for an intentional foul by the defence;
(d) To indicate the area in which a player can be offside.

Flag posts
Flag posts, at least 4 feet (1.2 m) high and not more than 5 feet (1.5 m), are placed one each corner, and one at the centre of each side line at least one yard outside the line. They must not be removed during the game.

Equipment

Sticks

The stick is made of wood (ash or mulberry), the handle (cane) usually having one or more layers of rubber inserted along its length. The handle is bound tightly and usually has a covering to give a non-slip hand grip. The head, which is spliced into the handle, has a flat face on the left-hand side (holding the stick correctly for play), and is curved on the other side.

The weight must not exceed 28 oz (794 g), nor be less than 12 oz (340 g), and the stick must be thin enough for a ring having an interior diameter of 2 inches (5.1 cm) to pass over the whole length.

The head of the stick must not have any insets, edgings, or fittings of hard wood or other substance, and sharp edges and splinters are not allowed. Surgical tape can be bound round the head to prevent splintering, providing the stick can still be passed through a 2-inch ring. On no account must the blade of the stick be cut square or be pointed, as this would make play dangerous.

Ball

A ball of any material or colour, sewn or seamless, but of the correct weight and size, may be used as agreed mutually before the game. The weight should be between $5\frac{1}{2}$ and $5\frac{3}{4}$ oz (156–163 g). The circumference of the ball should not be more than $9\frac{1}{4}$ inches (23.5 cm) and not less than $8\frac{13}{16}$ inches (22.4 cm).

Uniform

To ensure that players are tidily and suitably dressed for the game, the A.E.W.H.A. has laid down the following rules for the uniform to be worn:

'All players shall wear skirts or divided skirts; the goalkeeper, however, may wear trousers; skirts and divided skirts shall not be more than 9 inches or less than 3 inches off the ground when the player kneels. Either long or three-quarter length stockings must be worn. Tights, if worn, shall be of a natural colour. Goalkeepers shall wear a colour different from that of their own team and that of their opponents.'

Team uniform

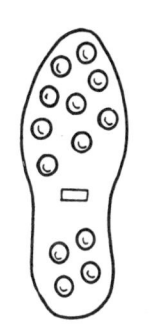

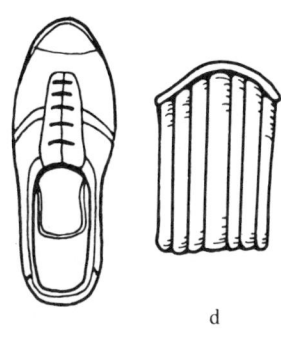

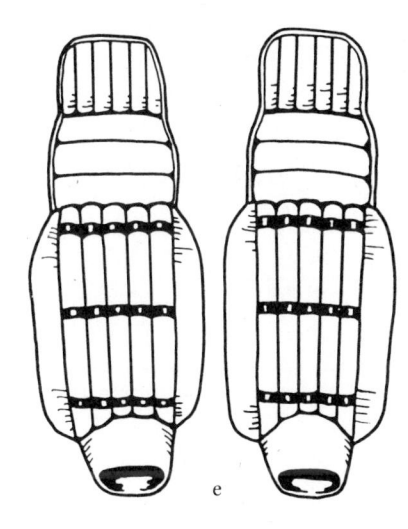

Shin guards may be worn.

To prevent any possibility of injury, players must not wear metal badges or anything of a similar nature.

Footwear
Shoes should have soles suitable for the playing surface, so it is advisable to find out before a match what kind of surface you will be playing on. Metal spikes, dangerous studs and protruding nails are prohibited.

Goalkeeper's equipment
Goalkeepers may wear additional protective equipment including special pads of cane or like cricket pads, kickers, gauntlets, body protectors (which must be worn under shirt or jacket), headgear, face masks and elbow pads.

The umpires
Umpires should carry:
   a current rule book;
   a good whistle with a wrist cord;
   two pencils;
   a stop watch, or a reliable watch with a second hand;
   a card on which to record the score;
   a set of misconduct cards (see p. 23).

The rules make no stipulation concerning the dress of the umpires, but the

Footwear (a and b are suitable for an artificial pitch, studs (c) for grass); shin guard (d) and goalkeeper's pads

following are recommended by the umpires' sub-committee:

(a) Suitable clothing allowing free movement and of a different colour from those worn by either of the teams;

(b) Footwear similar to that of the players, appropriate to the playing surface.

Rules of play

Duration of game

A game is divided into two periods of 35 minutes each, unless otherwise agreed before the game, with a half-time period after which the teams change ends. The interval should not normally exceed 5 minutes, although this may be extended if agreed before the start of the match.

In all games the umpires should note the time lost for any enforced stoppage, e.g. penalty stroke or accident, and add this time to the end of the half in which the stoppage occurred. Players and umpires should endeavour to keep such time to a minimum.

Choice of ends

It is customary for the captains of the two teams to meet with the umpires, and for the home captain to toss a coin, giving the visitor the call. The captain winning the toss may choose either (i) which end to attack in the first half, or (ii) possession of the ball at the start of the game. The winner having made her choice, the opposing team automatically has the second option.

Starting and restarting the game

The pass-back
The game is started, and restarted after half-time and after each goal, by a pass-back from the centre of the pitch. The pass-back at the beginning of the game is taken by the team which did not make a choice of ends, and by the opposing team after half-time; after a goal the game is restarted by the team against whom the goal was scored.

For the pass-back, the ball is placed on the centre spot and all players, other than the striker, take up their positions in their own half of the field. No member of the team without possession may be within 5 yards (4.57 m) of the ball.

The pass-back may be hit or pushed, and must be directed into the defending half of the field. Having taken the pass-back, the striker must not play the ball again nor approach within playing distance, until it has been touched by another player of either team. Time-wasting is not allowed.

The bully
A bully is taken to restart the game after certain stoppages, e.g. an accident not caused by a foul, the ball lodging in a goalkeeper's pad or in the clothing of another player or an umpire, or any unforeseen incident such as a dog interfering with the game. The bully is taken on a spot chosen by the umpire in whose half the incident occurred; a bully in the circle must not be taken within 5 yards of the goal/back line.

To take the bully, a player from each team stands squarely facing the side line, left shoulder towards the goal she is attacking, with the ball on the ground between them. Each player taps the ground behind the ball, and then, with the flat face of the stick, taps her opponent's stick above the ball, three times alternately before attempting to play the ball. The bully is completed and the ball in play when it has been touched by one of the players taking the bully. Until the bully is completed, all other players must be nearer their back line than the ball, and at least 5 yards from the ball.

Ball in and out of play

A ball is in play until it has passed wholly over the side lines or goal/back lines even though the player playing the ball may herself be outside the playing area.

The ball is not out of play if it rebounds off the umpire (standing on the field of play) or off the goal-post, crossbar, or corner flag into the field of play.

The push-/hit-in

When the whole of the ball passes over either side line off the stick of a player, it is pushed or hit in, in any direction from the point where it crossed the line.

The ball is still in play if it is on or inside the line, even though the player is outside the playing area

Preparing to take a hit-in from the side line

The rules state that:

(a) The push-/hit-in must be taken by an opponent of the player who last touched the ball before it crossed over the side line.

(b) The ball must be pushed or hit. It must not be lifted deliberately nor rise dangerously. The striker must move the ball—just to touch it with her stick is not sufficient.

(c) The ball must be placed on the line at the point where it crossed the line.

(d) No player of the opposing team shall be within 5 yards of the ball.

(e) The striker shall not play the ball again, nor remain or approach within playing distance of the ball, until it has been touched by another player of either team. The player taking the push- or hit-in may stand in the field of play.

If the umpire considers that a player is deliberately standing nearer than 5 yards to delay the push- or hit-in, she need not stop the game.

Penalties for infringements

For any breach of the rule a free hit is awarded to the opposing team.

If the umpire considers an offence by a defender in her own 25 yards area to be deliberate, she may award a penalty corner.

16 yard hit-out

When the ball is sent out of play over the back line by a player of the attacking team and no goal is scored, or if the ball is, in the umpire's opinion, unintentionally sent over the back line by one of the defending team from a distance of 25 yards or more, play is restarted by a hit or push taken by one of the defending team exactly opposite the place where the ball crossed the back line, not more than 16 yards from the inner edge of that line.

The ball must be stationary before it is hit or pushed. It must not be raised intentionally. It must be moved from its original position; just touching it with the stick is not deemed to be a hit.

The opposing team must be at least 5 yards from the ball. Having taken the hit-out, the striker must not play the ball again nor remain or approach within playing distance until it has been touched by another player of either team.

A race for possession of the ball

A push or hit from the back line

A push or hit from the back line is awarded to the attacking team when the whole of the ball, having last been played by one of the defending team within the 25 yards area, passes unintentionally out of play behind the back line.

Regulations concerning a push or hit from the back line:

(a) The hit or push is taken by one of the attacking team. In doing so, the striker must move the ball from its original position.

(b) The ball must be motionless on the back line within 5 yards of the corner flag.

(c) All players of the defending team must be at least 5 yards from the ball.

(d) Should the striker raise the ball deliberately or dangerously, approach it or play it again before anyone else has touched it, a free hit is awarded to the defence.

(e) While the ball need not be stopped before a shot at goal is made, any shot which is in itself dangerous or could lead to dangerous play will be penalised.

Note: In order to make the best use of a hit-out, it should be taken without delay, but with due regard for the 5 yards rule.

Scoring a goal

The scoring of goals is the object of the game—the team scoring the most goals is the winner of the match. If no goals or an equal number of goals are scored, the game is a draw.

Regulations concerning the scoring of a goal:

(a) The whole of the ball must pass over the goal line between the posts and under the cross-bar.

(b) The ball must have been hit by, or glanced off, the stick of an attacking player in the circle. If, after having been hit by an attacker in the circle, the ball comes into contact with the person or stick of a defender and then enters the goal, a goal is scored.

(c) Should the goal post and/or the cross-bar collapse, the umpire must use her judgement and if she considers the ball crossed the line between and under where the posts and bar should have been, she will award a goal.

Reverse stick dribble—ball must not be played with rounded side of stick

Fouls

Fouls are largely the result of faulty stickwork, footwork, or positioning of the body. For penalties see page 22. The fouls may be divided into eight categories, as follows.

Dangerous play

(a) A ball above the height of the shoulder must not be played with any part of the stick.

A player must not raise her stick in such a way that it endangers, intimidates, or hampers another player when she plays or attempts to play the ball, approaches it or stops it.

(b) A player must not hit the ball in such a way that it rises dangerously or may lead to dangerous play. A scoop which raises the ball in a controlled manner is permissible; however, any pass made into the circle must not be raised deliberately. Elsewhere on the pitch a lifted ball which is dangerous, either in flight or on landing, will be penalised.

A dangerous, intimidating stroke

Illegal stick tackle

However, opponents who approach within 5 yards of a player receiving a high ball will be considered to be creating a dangerous situation and penalised accordingly.

It is totally prohibited to lift the ball from the ground and hit it again while still in the air.

(c) A player who hits wildly into an opponent will be penalised for dangerous play.

Backsticks

A player must not hit the ball with the rounded side of her stick. This is a common fault with beginners when attempting to hit the ball on their left side. If the ball merely hits the back of the stick and no advantage results, no offence has taken place.

Interference

A player must not strike, hit, hook, hold or interfere in any way with her opponent's stick.

For example, a defender may not hold down an attacker's stick with her own.

Handling the ball

The ball may be moved with the stick only; a player must not stop the ball with her hand either on the ground or in the air, nor may she catch it (see goalkeeper's privileges, p. 19).

A player who uses her hand to protect herself from a dangerously raised ball will not be penalised.

Kicking the ball

A player must not kick the ball or use her feet to support the stick when she is tackled by an opponent. Stopping the ball with the foot counts as kicking.

It is not necessarily a foul if the ball strikes the foot and there is no advantage.

Handling opponents

A player must not trip, shove, push, charge, strike at, or in any way personally handle her opponent.

Example: if the defender, by pushing her stick just in front of the attacker, trips her up, she commits a foul.

A player must not push or in anyway personally handle her opponent

17

Obstruction: a player must not run between an opponent and the ball

Pushing
Example: if the attacker has over-run the ball and the defender, close behind, accidentally pushes her forward and prevents her regaining it, the defender commits a foul.

Charging
Example: if the defender attempts to force the attacker away from the ball by charging with her shoulder.

Obstruction
A player must not obstruct by running between an opponent and the ball, if that opponent is within playing distance, nor interpose any part of her body or her stick between another player and the ball in such a way that her opponent does not have a fair chance of playing the ball.

Interference without stick
A player must not interfere in the game in any way unless she has her stick in her hand.

Example: if the goalkeeper has dropped her stick and continues to defend her goal without stick in hand, she is fouling.

Goalkeeper's privileges

While the ball is in her circle the goalkeeper may kick the ball and stop it with any part of her body, including her hand. She is also allowed latitude with balls which rebound from her body or hand, but she is not allowed to strike at the ball with her hand, nor to throw it.

She may wear protective equipment (see page 9), but wearing this does not mean that she may behave in a way which would not be safe without that protection. Should she do so, she may be penalised.

Provided it does not cause undue delay, she may put on protective equipment or remove headgear, mask and gloves at a penalty stroke or penalty corner.

These privileges are transferred if another team member changes roles with the goalkeeper (see page 3).

The goalkeeper may wear protective equipment, and has other privileges in the circle

Offside

As in many field games where scoring is by means of goals, some restrictions are applied to prevent players gaining an advantage by lingering near the opponents' goal ready to score from short range. This restricting rule is known as the Offside Rule and some players find it difficult to understand.

As the infringement of this rule causes an immediate breakdown of the attack and gives a free hit to the defending team it is necessary that all its details should be clearly understood.

Stated in full, the rule says:

'AT THE MOMENT WHEN THE BALL IS PLAYED, a player of the same team as the striker is offside if she is in her opponents' 25 yards area, unless she is behind the ball or there are at least two opponents nearer their back line than she is.

She should not be penalised unless she is gaining any advantage from being or having been in an offside position.'

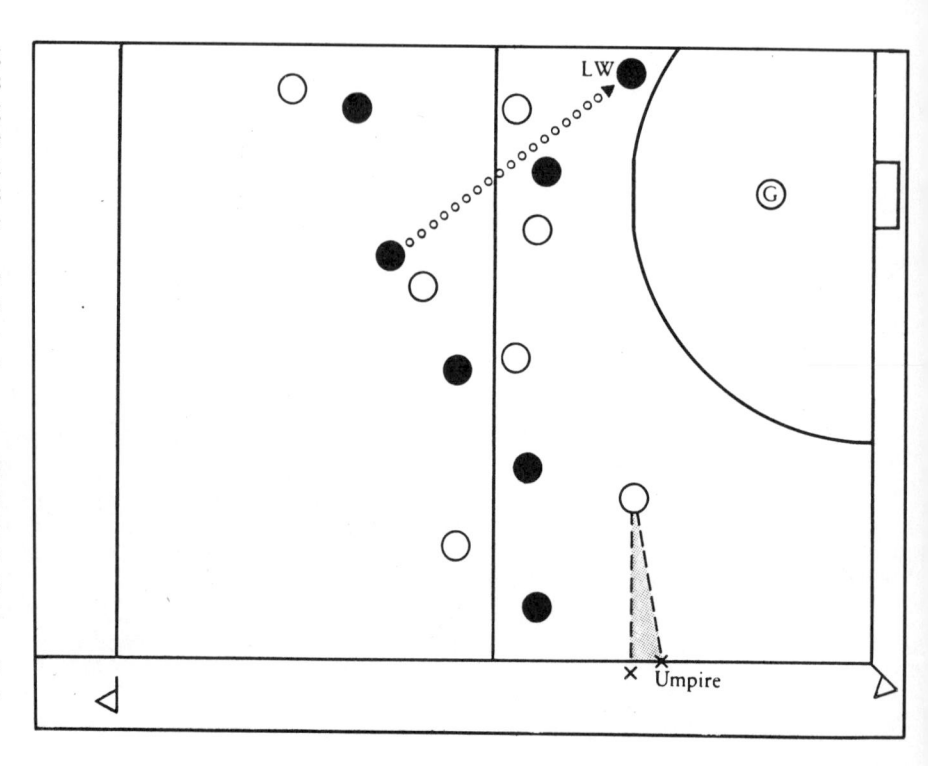

The important factor is the player's position when the ball is played, not when she receives it.

Penalty for offside: a free hit is awarded to the defending team.

Examples

1. The Left Wing is offside because, when the ball was last played, there was only one defender between her and the back line.

Position of umpire: The umpire is level with or slightly nearer the back line than the second defender.

Key
○ ○ ○ ○ ▶ = movement of ball
▬ ▪ ▬ ▶ = movement of player
Shaded area shows recommended position of umpire

◀ Example 1: Left Wing is offside

2. The Left Inner is offside in the circle because, when the ball was hit, there was only one defender, the goalkeeper, between her and the back line.

The umpire has closed in, in order to see more clearly in the congested circle, and is still level with, or slightly ahead of, the second defender.

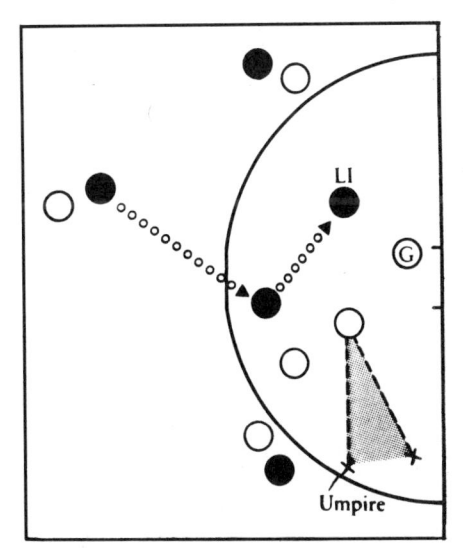

Example 2: Left Inner offside

3. The Right Wing is offside because, when the ball was hit, she was in her opponents' 25 yard area and there was only one defender, the goalkeeper, between her and the back line.

The umpire is at the 25 yards line to see whether the other forwards cross the line before the centre forward hits the ball, making them offside.

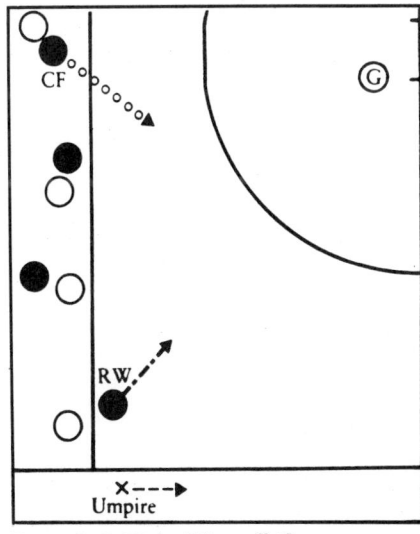

Example 3: Right Wing offside

21

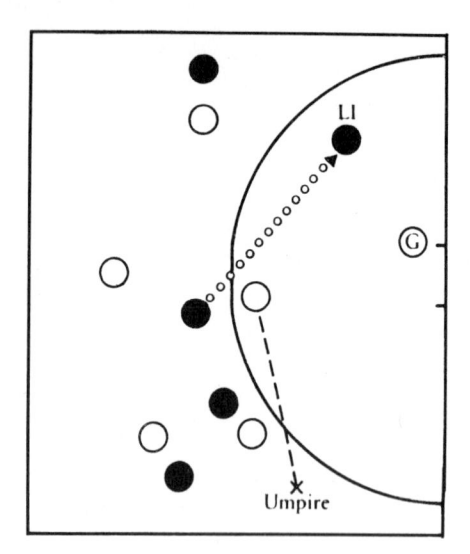

Example 4: Left Inner offside

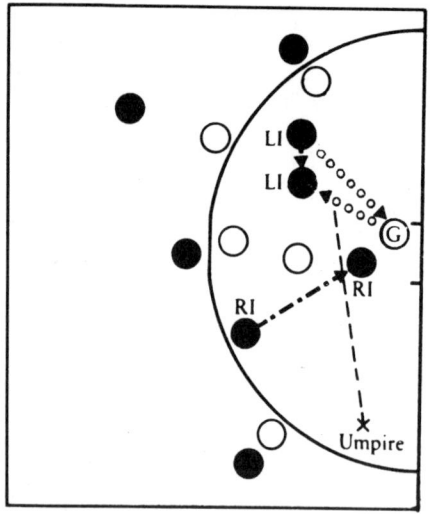

Example 5: Right Inner offside

4. The Left Inner is offside because the defenders have been left behind and, when the ball was hit, there was only the goalkeeper between her and the back line.

The umpire is slightly ahead of the second defender.

5. Left Inner shoots and follows up.

The goalkeeper clears the ball towards her and so she shoots again.

The Right Inner is then offside because, having rushed the Left Inner's first shot, she failed to get back onside before the Left Inner shot again.

The umpire has closed in, and should be level with the ball.

Penalties

Penalties can be grouped under three headings:

(a) Penalty stroke when a defender intentionally breaks a rule in the circle or in any case when a goal most probably would have been scored but for the breaking of the rule;

(b) Penalty corners for fouls committed by defenders in the circle or by offenders inside their own 25 yards area if the umpire is satisfied that an offence has been deliberate;

(c) Free hits for all fouls other than defence fouls in the circle and deliberate infringements in the defending 25 yards area.

In addition to the above penalties, the umpire has the power to warn or suspend any player or players guilty of serious misconduct or rough or dangerous play; this may be done by showing a coloured disciplinary card:

Green indicates a warning;
Yellow indicates temporary suspension for not less than 5 minutes;
Red indicates suspension for the remainder of the match.

Penalty stroke

A penalty stroke is awarded for an intentional foul by a defender in the circle or if a probable goal is prevented by a defence foul. A penalty stroke may also be awarded if defenders persistently cross the line too soon at penalty corners. The time needed for taking the stroke is added on to that half.

Procedure

The penalty stroke is taken by a player nominated by the attacking team from a spot 7 yards in front of the centre of the goal line; the ball may be flicked, scooped or pushed at any height. The striker may take one step forward, though her back foot must not pass her front foot before the ball is moved. She is not allowed to follow up her shot.

The stroke is defended by the goalkeeper on the pitch at the time, unless she is incapacitated or suspended, in

Goal scored from penalty stroke

23

Corner: up to five defenders may stand behind goal/back line

which case a substitute is nominated, who may don protective equipment. She must stand with both feet on the goal line, and after the umpire has blown the whistle must not move either foot before the ball is struck. She retains her usual privileges.

All other players must be beyond the 25 yard line and should stand towards the sides of the pitch, not in the goalkeeper's line of vision.

The umpire in control of the stroke must be able to see both players and the goal. An advantageous position is slightly behind and to the right of the striker. It is general practice for the other umpire to stand on the back line to check whether the ball has crossed the goal line, e.g. the goalkeeper catching it with her hand behind the goal line.

Completion

A goal is scored if the ball crosses the goal line; a penalty goal is awarded if a foul by the goalkeeper prevents the ball entering the goal.

The stroke is completed and the game restarted by a 16 yard hit in front of the centre of the goal if the ball passes out of the circle or comes to rest in the circle. A ball caught by the goalkeeper or lodged in her pads is considered to be 'at rest'.

If the attacker fouls, the stroke is over and the game restarts with a 16 yard hit. Taking the stroke before the whistle is blown, feinting at striking the ball or any deliberate action which induces the goalkeeper to move her feet are regarded as fouls.

Penalty corner

A penalty corner is awarded for an unintentional defence foul in the circle, or if a defender fouls intentionally in the 25 yards area or deliberately hits the ball over the back line.

Rules concerning a penalty corner:
(a) The hit is taken on whichever side the attack chooses, at a point not less than 10 yards from the nearer goal-post.
(b) The ball must be on the back line and be hit or pushed by an attacker; it must not be lifted deliberately nor rise dangerously.
(c) Apart from the striker, all

This tackle could easily lead to a stick obstruction

England players watch the ball closely as they follow up a penalty corner

members of the attacking team must be on the field of play, at least 5 yards from the ball and must have their feet and sticks outside the circle.

(d) Not more than five of the defending team—it may be any five—must stand behind their back line (feet and sticks) and at least 5 yards from the ball; the remainder of the team must stand beyond the centre line.

(e) If players from either team move into the circle before the ball is hit, the umpire may require the hit to be retaken.

(f) If the striker approaches or plays the ball again before anyone has touched it, a free hit is awarded to the defence.

(g) Unless the ball has been touched by a defender, an attacker must stop it before she shoots. If one player stops the ball and then passes, a fellow attacker may shoot directly; but if a pass or deflection has been made without the ball being stopped, the second player must stop it before shooting.

(h) The first hit at goal must not cross the goal line above the height of the side-boards/back board (18 inches, 45.7 cm) unless it has touched the stick or person of a defender. Scoop and flick shots are allowed, provided that they cause no danger.

(i) No goal can be scored directly by the player taking the penalty corner.

(j) If the ball travels more than 5 yards beyond the outer edge of the circle, the penalty corner is deemed to be over and the ball in normal play. Although there is then no requirement for the ball to be stopped, any stroke or shot is subject to the dangerous play rule (see page 15).

Free hit

Points to remember:

(a) All players of the opposing team must be at least 5 yards from the ball. However, for a free hit to the attacking team within 5 yards of the circle, players of both teams, apart from the striker, must be 5 yards from the ball.

(b) The ball must be stationary and must be hit or pushed. A scoop or flick is not allowed; a free hit must not be lifted deliberately nor must the ball rise dangerously.

(c) The player taking the hit must

Moving to take a free hit; all opposing players are at least 5 yards from the ball

not play the ball again until it has been touched by another player, nor may she approach or remain within playing distance of the ball.

(d) If the player hits at but misses the ball, the stroke may be taken again by her.

(e) The ball must be moved; it is not sufficient for the striker to tap the top of the ball before a team-mate makes use of it.

(f) For infringements by the player taking the hit, a free hit is awarded to the other side.

The free hit is taken on the spot where the infringement occurred—*but* if a free hit is awarded to the defending team within the 16 yards area it may be taken from any spot within this area on a line drawn parallel to the side line from where the foul occurred; and if the breach of the rule occurred within the circle the free hit may be taken anywhere within the circle if the player so wishes.

A player who gains extra advantage by taking the free hit in the wrong place should be penalised.

Control of the game

Umpires

Two umpires are responsible for the control of the game. They must know all the rules of the game thoroughly, and should be capable of applying them. Quite often a decision rests upon the umpire's opinion. Was the ball sent over the back line intentionally or not? Is a player in an offside position interfering with the game? Is a particular stroke dangerous?

Each umpire controls half the field (the division being the centre line) for the whole game without changing ends. When standing on the side line facing into the field, the umpire is primarily responsible for decisions on the half of the field on her right. It is customary that there is an imaginary diagonal from one 25 yard line to the other, and in this quarter each umpire deals with fouls coming towards her from the other circle. Each umpire gives decisions on the hit-in down the whole length of her side line and on fouls in the 5 yards area; she is wholly responsible for decisions on back line hits, penalty corners, penalty strokes and goals in her half, and free hits in her circle.

An umpire's duties are:

(a) To enforce the rules, subject to the advantage rule, i.e. that the umpire should refrain from penalising in cases where she is satisfied that by doing so she would be giving an advantage to the offending team.

For example, an attacking player, although being obstructed near the circle, may still be able to press home the attack and make a shot at goal; should the umpire penalise the obstruction and award a free hit, the defenders would be able to recover and mark their opponents closely.

(b) To stop the game for an infringement, awarding the appropriate penalty indicated by an arm signal. In the case of misconduct or rough or dangerous play, the umpire has the power to warn or suspend the offending player as well as penalising her. The umpire may also stop play if an accident or any unforeseen incident makes this necessary.

(c) To whistle to indicate the resumption of play after a stoppage.

(d) To act as timekeeper and allow the full or agreed time. By agreement one umpire is primarily responsible for starting and ending each half, but it is essential that both umpires check the time. Time taken for a penalty stroke is added to the half in which it occurred, also any time lost for accidents or other enforced stoppages. The umpire controls the time for any suspensions.

(e) To keep a written record of the goals scored.

Umpire's position on the field

(a) Each umpire controls the same half of the field for the whole game; when facing the pitch the goal in her half of the field is on her right. She is also responsible for fouls in the diagonal area (see over).

(b) The offside rule is a question of alignment of players, which can only

If the umpire is close to the play, the players will more readily accept her decision

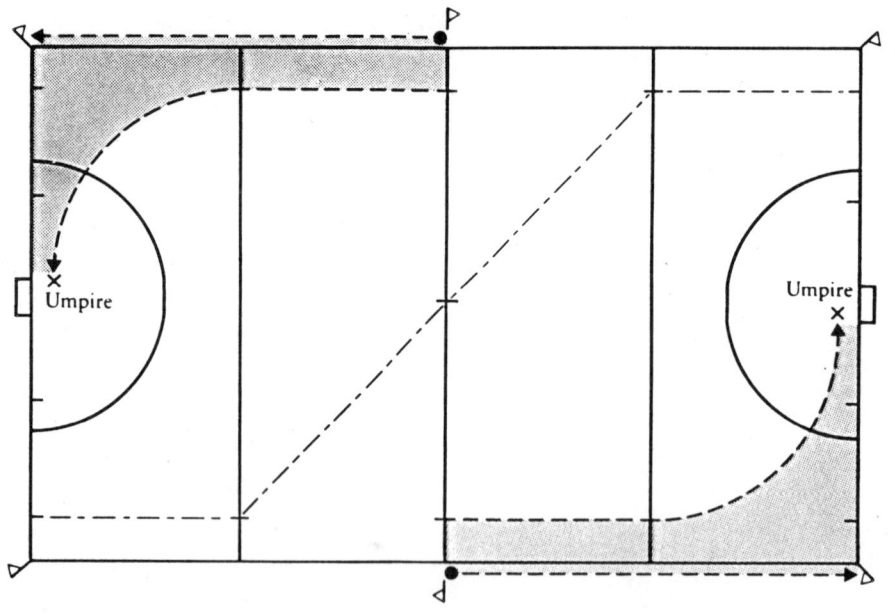

Umpires' positions
The shaded area shows the approximate range of movement; the diagonal line, the division of responsibility

be judged correctly by viewing the play at right angles to the side line; as play comes into her 25 yards area the umpire should be level with or slightly nearer the back line than the second defender or the foremost attacking player. Thus any attacker on her right is in an offside position.

(c) The umpire should keep outside the field of play between the centre line and the 25 yard line, moving up and down to ensure a clear view of play. From the 25 yard line she should move in towards the nearer goal post so that she can see incidents in the circle. She must be ready to move out quickly if play swings towards her side line to avoid impeding players or allowing the ball to go out of sight behind her. The umpire's path roughly resembles the shape of a hockey stick.

At all times she must be able to see the ball.

Timekeepers

It is permissible to have timekeepers; it is recommended that two be appointed and that they stay on one side of the field.

Their duties are:

(a) To take the time when the umpire starts each half.

(b) To note any time lost for penalty strokes and any enforced stoppages, and add this to the half in which they occur.

(c) To blow the whistle for half-time and full-time.

Technical tables

At most International and Territorial matches and National Championships, technical tables are used. The judges at the technical table keep a complete record of the match; the report sheet shows the names of the squads and umpires, indicating any substitutions which are made. The goal scorers' names are recorded with the time and whether the goal was the outcome of a penalty corner or penalty stroke, or from open play.

The judges are responsible for timekeeping; they take the time from the umpire's whistle at the start and sound their hooter for the end of each half, adding the necessary time for penalty strokes and stoppages to the half in which they occur.

The table controls all substitutions with the assistance of the umpire, recording the time when they take place. Disciplinary cards given to any player(s) are also recorded, along with the time.

Good defensive play by the Canadian team in response to an English attack

Questions

The pages on which the answers to these questions will be found are given in brackets.

1. Is it permissible for a member of the team to change places with the goalkeeper? (page 3)
2. Where must all players be for a pass-back? (page 5)
3. May the goalkeeper kick the ball when she is outside the circle? (pages 7 and 19)
4. How high should goal-posts be? (page 7)
5. May players wear metal badges and brooches? (page 9)
6. If a dog runs off with the ball, how is the game restarted, and where? (page 10)
7. When is the ball in play after a bully? (page 11)
8. If the ball hits the goal-posts and rebounds, should play go on? (page 11)
9. May the ball be lifted at a push-in? (page 12)
10. What happens when the ball passes over the back line off the stick of an attacker? (page 13)
11. May a player take a flying shot at goal following a hit from the back line? (page 14)
12. May a player strike a ball above shoulder height with any part of her stick? (page 15)
13. Is it permissible to hit the ball with the rounded part of the stick? (page 16)
14. May a player interfere with her opponent's stick? (page 16)
15. A player accidentally kicks the ball—is this allowed? (page 17)
16. Can a player be offside between the centre and the 25 yard line? (page 20)
17. From where is a penalty corner taken? (page 25)
18. Must the ball be stationary at a free hit? (page 27)
19. Which part of the field has each umpire under her control? (page 28)
20. What extra time does an umpire allow for a penalty stroke? (page 29)

32